Foreword

BY PAUL KAVANAGH (WEE GINGER DUG)

The Pulitzer prize-winning American journalist David Remnick, editor of The New Yorker magazine, once said that 98% of people who get the magazine say that they read the cartoons first, and the other 2% are lying. The Scottish independence campaign of 2014 brought a whole range of characters to public prominence, characters who made us think, who made us laugh, and who subtly or not so subtly undermined the basis of British rule in Scotland. One of the most influential was a cartoon lion called Hamish, the inspired creation of Chris Cairns. Hamish is, after a certain not really that wee ginger dug, my favourite Scottish independence animal. Week after bruising week in the independence campaign, you always knew that Hamish would be there for you on Wings Over Scotland of a weekend, putting it all into perspective in a wry and amusing manner. Through Hamish, Chris would give you a laugh, and would leave you with a wee smile that lasted the rest of the day. Nothing seemed so bad after that.

Despite the predictions of the frothier elements in the No camp, the independence movement didn't go away after September 2014. Scotland changed forever in that summer of 2014. We were no longer a country that was content to accept the status quo, resigned to the belief that we could never change things. A good cartoon can illustrate that change in an image that lasts in the mind in a way that all the wordy text in the world can never do. My favourite cartoons of Chris's are the two he published in the immediate aftermath of that September vote, the first showing a male hand in a shirt cuff fastened with a Union flag cufflink snuffing out a candle marked "hope", followed a couple of days later by a drawing of Hamish's paw holding a lit match. That's the thing about hope – once you learn how to hope it's a lesson you never unlearn. And in that summer of 2014 this cynical nation of Scotland had learned how to hope. Chris and Hamish summed it up perfectly. His cartoons keep that flame of hope burning. The match is still burning bright.

The independence movement isn't going away. A cartoon lion helped to take the idea of Scottish independence from the margins of politics and didn't just make it mainstream – the question of independence is now the central pivot around which all of Scottish politics revolves. We're no longer arguing about whether Scotland should become an independent country; we're arguing about when. In the teeth of the concerted opposition of the entire British establishment, in the face of the contempt of the overwhelming majority of the traditional media, the people of Scotland achieved that.

We achieved it with words, with jokes, with humour. We achieved it with Greg Moodie's surreal take on surreal politics, with the snarky snarls of a wee ginger dug, with the analysis of bloggers, writers, campaigners, and with the pointed and perfectly aimed cartoons of Chris Cairns featuring Hamish the lion. We can be sure that Hamish will be with us on every step of the journey as Scotland completes the transition set in train in that summer of 2014 and once again takes its place amongst the independent nations of this world. Brexit has exposed the chasm between Scotland and the British state, a chasm that grows ever wider. Hamish the lion shines a light into that chasm. One day, sooner than we might think, Scotland will be an independent nation again, and when it is, we'll have our own stamps. One of those stamps will feature a cartoon lion called Hamish.

Some people don't like political cartoons, generally those people who are the targets of their barbs. Apparently, the right of the powerful not to be offended is greater than the right of the rest of us to laugh at the pretensions and hypocrisy of the powerful. Even Chris's gentle, human and humane cartoons have been criticised by some for being offensive and disrespectful. But a respectful political cartoon is no longer a political cartoon; it's just a drawing that says nothing and has no message. Chris has a message, and it's a message that he never shies away from.

The powerful don't like cartoons and satire because laughter can change the world in a way that anger can't. When you laugh at the powerful it means you're no longer afraid of them, and when you're no longer afraid of them they no longer have any power over you. Chris's cartoons are a weekly exercise in bursting the bubble of Scotland's Unionist establishment, an establishment that has had its own way for far too long, an establishment which knows that its days are numbered. Chris and Hamish will keep us laughing and thinking all the way to independence, and beyond.

"VANITY PROJECT"...

...VANITY PROJECTILE.

Introduction

It is the job of political cartoonists to focus on the hypocritical and mendacious, the sleazy and, occasionally, the grim. Sorry about that – but it's all in the good and noble cause of lampoonery. I hope therefore, that despite the following collection of hucksters, liars and actual murderers, despite these reminders of tragedies and farce, you will find much to enjoy in this, the second volume of my cartoons.

As with the first, it isn't offered as a two-year course in modern history – if only because it is heavily focused on Scotland and unapologetically partisan. You will look here in vain for any easy pot shots at the Scottish government or wider independence movement. Greg Moodie (m'publisher) and I have done a few speaking gigs over the last year or so and a common question is: 'Why do you never attack the SNP?' To which the short answer is that we'd love to. But, not only would we struggle to be seen and heard amid the pitchfork and torch-wielding media mob constantly baying for Nat blood, we see nothing wrong in picking a side. After all, that's exactly what the vast majority of Scotland's newspapers and broadcasters have done. At least we're honest enough to admit it.

In an ideal world, I would love this collection to include jokes at the SNP's expense, to challenge power without fear or favour. In an ideal world, an underperforming government in Edinburgh would be in my sights every week, its shortcomings fair game. But in an ideal world that Edinburgh would be a proper capital and Scotland would be independent. Until it is, the power that needs challenging – and rarely is by the traditional media – is the British state and its ongoing efforts to crush Scottish self-determination. They don't need and won't get my help.

Scotland, and the 'national question', therefore remain front and centre in this collection. But every now and then, like everyone else, I've stopped and gaped open-mouthed at what was going on beyond our shores. Two years ago, my theme for Volume I (Welcome to Cairnstoon) was living in 'interesting times'. We were a year beyond a referendum that had taken independence from minority interest to, well, a much bigger minority interest. The 45 per centers were a new and confident voice in the land, and the SNP had come within just 4,252 votes of winning every single Westminster seat in Scotland. It had been a wild ride, like a rollercoaster at the carnival. Little did we know it was just a warm-up for the circus.

Viewed from here, being one YouGov poll away from victory in September 2014 looks sort of normal, a bit ho-hum. The British establishment got a fright, yes, but then it did what it does best, what it's always done – made a pot of tea and pretended the entire beastly episode never happened. Well, it doesn't have that option any more. Because what's happened since is the sort of epochal shit that happens only once an epoch. It's that big.

As luck would have it, these pages cover a moment in history when the Anglo-American world said, 'Sod it,' stuck on a big red nose and started throwing custard pies around. Brexit and the election of Donald Trump are still, many months on, scarcely believable acts of anarchic lunacy – and one of them hasn't even happened yet. More than once I've sat over the blank sheet of paper at the end of the week and wondered how on Earth I could poke fun at a turn of real events that would have been rejected by the most acid of TV political satirists as too fanciful. Luckily, I've always had the antics of Mses Davidson and Dugdale, not to mention wee Willie Rennie, to fall back on.

So, my thanks to them for the endless and rich supply of material. Also to the Rev Stuart Campbell at Wings Over Scotland (and, for a while at least, Mike Small at Bella Caledonia) for publishing my cartoons on those rare weeks when I'm not on holiday. With due respect to others in the field, Wings continues to be the most relevant and trenchant pro-independence voice on the web and I'm proud to do the colouring in for it.

Thanks are also due, as per, to Greg for his invaluable help in turning my doodles and scribblings into a proper book, and to Paul Kavanagh, aka Wee Ginger Dug, for doing me the honour of writing a foreword. Speaking of top columnists, I am also indebted to Robert McNeil, one of Scotland's foremost spellers, for his editing.

Most of all, however, I'd like to thank you the readers for buying this book (obviously) and every Saturday showing your appreciation for my Friday labours. It almost makes missing a day on the golf course worth it.

Deterrent-proof

The hoary old issue of Trident, the US nuclear missile system Britain gets to buy and pretend it controls, reared its head during the Labour leadership contest (you know, the first one when everyone was laughing at the old bloke from Steptoe & Son). While the likes of Andy Burnham said it would be his patriotic duty to press the button, Corbyn stuck to his old CND principles and demurred – thereby instantly ruining *cough* any faint chance he had of winning.

Not to be left out of the fun, Chancellor of the Exchequer George Osborne announced that several months before any decision by Parliament to actually renew the thing, Faslane would get a half a billion pound makeover. No reason. Not pre-empting anything, you understand. Just, you know, because it's worth it – what with intercontinental ballistic missiles being so useful against terrorists and cockroaches.

All obscenely expensive enough but given that added dash of tacky by taking place in the month of the 70th anniversary of the bombing of Hiroshima and Nagasaki.

Stuff your huddled masses

Speaking of cockroaches, such was the description of Syrian refugees by Sun columnist and five-times winner of the First to be Eaten Award by Crash Survivors' Weekly magazine, Katie Hopkins.

The European refugee crisis was now worsening by the day with heartbreaking stories and footage provoking calls for a commensurate response from elected leaders across the continent. While Greece and Italy, on the front line, redoubled their efforts to provide a safe welcome to the streams of refugees risking their lives to cross the Mediterranean, other nations immediately began organising transports, accommodation and every other logistical necessity in preparation for receiving this tidal wave of desperate, traumatised families.

By the end of the year, Germany was on track to have taken in a total of 1 million. The likes of Sweden, Hungary and the Netherlands were also taking in quota-busting numbers under an EU scheme the UK had, of course, managed to opt out of.

David Cameron's offer of spare capacity at the caravan park in Frinton (off season only) looked just a little less generous by comparison.

SORRY, BUT WE'RE OVERCROWDED AS IT IS. YOU WOULDN'T UNDERSTAND.

The Fifth Horseman

Such was his lead in the polls for months beforehand there was absolutely no surprise when joke entrant Jeremy Corbyn won the leadership of the Labour Party. This did not stop the leftish press from predicting a plague of boils followed swiftly by the end of civilisation as we know it, nor the Daily Mail from producing a joke greeting card edition that laughed out loud every time you turned a page.

But while the Tory Party began laying plans for a thousand-year Reich, there were more level-headed observers who weren't so alarmed. Common sense would prevail, they said. The normal rules of parliamentary party behaviour would be followed, they said. The Labour Party, they said, would get behind their new leader.

Which, to be fair, they did. With knives.

WHO'S THE NEW GUY?
FAMINE
WAR
DEATH
CONQUEST

A big boy did it and ran away

3 OCTOBER 2015

Labour's new leader horrified the Blairites by threatening to apologise on behalf of their party for taking the country into the Iraq War and killing hundreds of thousands of innocent civilians on a false premise. Imagine!

But he crapped out of it.

Instead, he and his 'top' team decided to deflect attention from their plummeting poll ratings at their annual conference with a spot of good old fashioned Nat-bashing. Except, being new at this sort of thing, they kind of got carried away. While John McDonnell, the newly appointed shadow chancellor, was rewriting parliamentary history and hoping no-one had heard of Hansard, his boss dropped a great deal of acid and then spoke.

The SNP, according to the putative PM, was in the process of privatising Calmac (really?), having had a wee practice when it privatised Scotrail. You remember that? In 1993? Before devolution? Disguised as John Major's Conservative government? Yeah, that. Sneaky Nat bastards.

I'VE NOW DECIDED NOT TO APOLOGISE FOR THE IRAQ WAR.
BUT THE SNP SHOULD...
...AND FOR THE POLL TAX...
...AND APPEASING HITLER.

One-Party Street

17 OCTOBER 2015

By the time the SNP got to hold their party conference in Aberdeen – the first since the 'tsunami' General Election – the other parties had had their own get-togethers, at which they all huddled down in the front few rows of mainly empty halls and moaned about living in a 'one-party state'.

So when the legions of the '45 swelled the rank and file of the SNP and the arena was packed to the rafters with cheering delegates, it was easy to see parallels with totalitarian regimes around the world.

After all, here was a governing party that had re-written the constitution to suit itself, forced apparatchiks into all spheres of everyday life, taken control of the national broadcast and print media, imprisoned opposition leaders and created a society in its own image enforced by fear and intimidation. All without ever once winning in a free and fair election.

Or something like that.

SIGH
WWW.CAIRNSTOON.COM
'15

Walking the dog

It being a month with an 'r' in it, it was time for Kezia Dugdale to unveil the latest Scottish Labour Autonomy Plan. A press conference was called, Allen keys were a-blur as the latest Labour modular exhibition stand was thrown up, a lectern assembled and the fold-down chairs laid out.

And everything went brilliantly. Until someone asked what it meant.

For example, what if the Scottish Labour conference agreed position a on policy x but the Labour Party Conference (you know, the real one) backed position b? What, indeed, if SLAB actually endorsed an entirely new policy, let's call it y, but the Labour Party preferred to leave y well alone because the Daily Mail would be mean to them?

'It's perfectly clear...' began Kez, and a roomful of eyes rolled skyward.

Handily, we didn't need to wait long for a concrete example of this new autonomy and clarity. Trident renewal is now opposed by the Scottish Labour Party but supported by its leader, taking her cue from the Labour Party Conference, despite that position being opposed by party leader Jeremy Corbyn, while its one Scottish MP, Ian Murray, who takes the PLP whip in Westminster, nevertheless opposes UK Party policy on the matter and agrees with SLAB. But not its leader. Who, according to the new autonomy plans (remember those?) is now his leader. Sort of.

Any questions?

Labour
SEE?
AUTONOMY!
CAIRNSTOON.COM/@CAIRNSTOON

Big girl's shoes

Kezia Dugdale was on a roll. Having established her divine right to rule the completely separate and independent branch of North British Labour (terms and conditions apply), she was now on a mission to revolutionise the arcane and outdated discipline of economics.

If little Johnnie has no apples but wants to give some to little Susie, he has to first get the apples from somewhere else, right? Wrong!

In Kezonomics, the apples – so long as they're not going to Susie but actually to some other much more deserving child – will magically appear out of thin air.

Thus the media spent a fruitless (geddit?) weekend trying to establish exactly how Scottish Labour would fund a £500 million tax credit boost out of money 'released' by not doing a thing the SNP said it might do, namely cut air passenger duty. Even the redoubtable Gordon Brewer gave up after several minutes of trying to nail jelly to a wall. Or 'interviewing Jackie Baillie' as it's sometimes known.

WHEN I'M FIRST MINISTER
I'LL SPEND ALL THE COUNTRY'S
MAGIC BEANS GOODER.
AND THERE'LL BE
FREE ICE CREAM
FOR EVERYBODY!

CAIRNSTOON.COM/@cairnstoon

Lies, damned lies
and political lies

14 NOVEMBER 2015

Leaky liar Alistair Carmichael MP was up before the beaks at a special electoral court hearing in Edinburgh to defend his right to hang onto his Orkney seat and his honour. He succeeded in one of those. Just.

He was taken to said court by four of his constituents, not for leaking a lie (Nicola Sturgeon's alleged preference for a Cameron win in the 2015 General Election), but for lying about the leak on TV ('The first I heard of this was when I got a phone call from a reporter'). And while he emerged with his reputation in tatters, he did achieve a first in quantum physics with some Nobel-standard hair-splitting.

His lie, he said, was an OK lie because it was a political lie told for political reasons, not a normal lie told for normal reasons, or, indeed political ones. As such it was not a lie that should have any bearing on his character … as a politician.

CAIRNSTOON. COM / @ cairnstoon
YOU'RE ABSOLUTELY SURE I STILL HAVE TO CALL HIM 'HONOURABLE' MEMBER?

Undesirables

Supporters of Scottish independence are often mischaracterised as believing in some sort of tartan supremacy – a notion that Scots are better than others, particularly the English. It is for this reason that polls and social attitudes surveys showing a minority of reactionary twats existing north of the Border are not, as the unionist media gleefully believe, a blow to the independence cause – quite the opposite in fact.

The only way Scotland is unique perhaps is that we house a significant number of people who believe we are incapable of running our own country.

But I digress. Proof, if it were needed, that some Scots are just as much of a dick as those of other nationalities came with a demonstration against asylum seekers by the Scottish Defence League in the Ayrshire village of Monkton. Not content with whipping up fear and hatred for any and all refugees, this fungus singled out "extra, secret, dark-skinned African males of the type who arrive in the country illegally from Calais and destroy their documents so there is no way to check if they have been murderers, rapists or paedophiles in their own country".

We can at least take some (national) pride in the fact that they were outnumbered three-to-one by a counter-demonstration of normal, sentient human beings.

WE SHOULDN'T LET THESE DANGEROUS EXTREMISTS INTO THE COUNTRY.
SDL
CAIRNSTOON.COM / @ cairnstoon

Cultivating terror

On the back of one of Europe's worst terrorist atrocities in living memory – the attacks on the Bataclan concert hall and other targets in Paris that left 130 dead – the declaration of 'war' on ISIS (Daesh) by President Hollande was perhaps understandable even if many feared it simply played into the hands of the murderous nutters.

But was there just a teensy bit of 'unfinished business' about David Cameron's rush to Hollande's call to arms? First he offered British military bases for the launch of French strikes then sought permission for the RAF itself to bomb targets in Syria. This, after all, was the Prime Minister who seriously misjudged the mood of Parliament in 2013 and lost a vote on bombing Assad's forces after his chemical attack on his own population.

The debate that followed (which he won) is remembered chiefly for the divisions it exposed within Jeremy Corbyn's shadow cabinet, but let's not forget the result was that the British, yet again, were getting involved in a conflict on foreign soil – an almost unbroken tradition stretching back 300 years.

CAIRNSTOON.COM/@cairnstoon

A bridge too far

Labour's desperate urge to blame the SNP government for absolutely anything that ever went wrong ever took a turn for the irrational a few weeks short of Christmas when a fault was found on the Forth Road Bridge. With barely a pause to find the cause or scale of the problem, Scottish Labour and their ever-loyal pals in the press screamed infamy at the government for putting lives at risk / closing the bridge / not closing the bridge / not spending enough money on repairs / not opening the bridge again / spending too much on the new bridge / not finishing the new bridge quickly enough. (Delete as applicable at any given time, multiple and contradictory choices allowed).

That the fault was unforeseen and unforeseeable, not the result of budget cuts and the closures necessary (all confirmed by those, until recently, actually in charge of the bridge and not SNP members or supporters) didn't matter.

Nor did the fact the new bridge that Labour complained was taking too long to finish was one they had done most to delay by opposing it tooth and nail for the thick end of 20 years.

SORRY MATE.
Labour
Sanctimonious Bullshit

Free bird seed

The recommendations of the Smith Commission, all but worthless though they were, faced just one last hurdle before being passed into law – agreeing the so-called fiscal framework that would determine how it would be paid for … and by whom.

Negotiations between the Scottish and UK governments were labyrinthine and almost important enough for Greg Hands, Chief Secretary to the Treasury, to cancel his holiday just days before the deadline. Almost, but not quite.

A particular sticking point was the principle of 'no detriment' – a commitment in the original Smith Commission report that the settlement should not adversely affect budgets north or south of the Border.

Needless to say, the Treasury tried to pull a fast one by suggesting a mechanism that would in fact have reduced the Scottish budget by around £3billion over ten years.

Luckily, the Scottish government's lead negotiator, John Swinney, doesn't do fast.

FISCAL FRAMEWORK
MORE POWERS
CAIRNSTOON.COM /@ cairnstoon.

Hairy prospects

27 FEBRUARY 2016

Viewed from here, the science fiction dystopia approach to dumb and dumber doesn't look quite so funny, does it? Indeed, it's difficult to remember a time when you could conjure up such a mad barnet formula safe in the knowledge that it would never – could never happen.

Boris as a way-in-the-future Tory leader was only being discussed because the bedraggled buffoon was positioning himself to take over from David Cameron who had already served notice he had fought his last General Election.

Meanwhile, Trump was nothing more than a curiously persistent presence in the seemingly endless marathon that is the US Presidential Election. As yet he hadn't even secured the Republican nomination but was fascinating pundits and public alike by being able to talk absolute horse-hockey without it appearing to put voters off.

Oh, if only we'd known …

Future
Shocks

Family values

5 MARCH 2016

David Cameron fired the starting pistol for the EU referendum. And shot himself in the foot. Having toured the capitals of Europe in search of a 'new deal' for Britain, he returned with hee-haw.

Nevertheless, having learned his lesson from the Scottish independence referendum, he would be accentuating the positive, selling the peace and prosperity of EU membership and leading the nation in a lusty chorus of I'd Like To Teach The World To Sing. Wouldn't he?

Unfortunately and unbeknownst to everyone (apart from a whole slew of celebrities who decided to die rather than hang about) the world had entered a parallel universe in 2016 – a universe in which the normal rules simply don't apply.

And so, despite the evidence of undiluted doom and gloom having almost doubled support for Scottish independence, Cameron and his remaining Tory pals launched straight into Project Fear Mk II. Genius.

PROJECT FEAR?
NONSENSE,
OLD MAN.
CAIRNSTOON.COM /@ cairnstoon

The passenger

On their calendars one suspects the date is ringed in red with perhaps a slurping tongue doodle to the side – so much do the Union Jocks look forward to GERS Day. Yes, it was that time of year again, time for another festival of too wee, too poor, too stupid for the self-haters. Oh, how they enjoy their annual fix of 'proof' their country's an economic basket case full of feckless dependents.

This year, the slump in the price of oil promised a bumper crop of devastating stats for the media to get their teeth into and, as sure as blindness follows drinking lighter fluid, our defenders of the truth duly ploughed on. This year's wizard wheeze in fact was comparing Scotland (unfavourably) with Greece.

The blindness, of course, was to inconvenient truths like the Scottish economy shrinking by less than 1%, despite the oil price crash. And truths like Scotland not actually having had any control over its economy for, oh … 300 years.

APPARENTLY, THE WORSE I GET AT DRIVING, THE MORE IT PROVES HOW BAD YOU WOULD BE AT IT. SEEMS FAIR.
G.E.R.S. 2014~2015
CAIRNSTOON.COM/@cairnstoon

Under his hat

The Panama Papers leak to The Guardian, Süddeutsche Zeitung and other international news organisations was as welcome in certain circles as a turd in a private swimming pool. There's little the leading tribunes of fair and open democracies dislike more than fair and open scrutiny of their conduct – especially if it shows them and their families behaving no better than the world's dodgiest despots.

Thus headlines about tax-avoiding on an industrial scale, using the kind of money-laundering offshore accounts favoured by drug barons and members of Take That, arrived with a thump on the oak desks of government offices from Iceland to Pakistan, Russia to South Africa. And they included details of a trust set up by David Cameron's old man.

Question: did junior invest in it? Answer came there none.

Well, not for several days. Finally, the Great Communicator coughed a fair bit, took a great deal of interest in some fluff on his sleeve and admitted he had indeed bought shares in the tax haven fund. But, he said brightly, he'd already sold it for a huge profit so everything now was perfectly fine.

HIDING? ME?
NOTHING.

On thee our hopes we fix

23 APRIL 2016

The 2016 Holyrood Election campaign rolled out across the country in a cavalcade of photo ops and soap box speeches in front of placard-waving rent-a-mobs.

Ruth Davidson climbed onto anything she could get her leg over, Kezia Dugdale put a brave face on … everything, and Willie Rennie, not to be outdone by Cameron's porcine peccadillos (alleged) was filmed in front of some shafting pigs saying, 'This sends a message about exactly what it is we're asking for'.

But apparently it was only the SNP who were indulging in personality politics – only Nicola Sturgeon who was being presented in presidential style. Maybe something to do with her not making a complete arse of herself on camera? Who knows.

Meanwhile, a rich old lady got older.

NICOLA
UGH! THAT SORT OF FAWNING SYCOPHANCY HAS NO PLACE IN BRITISH SOCIETY.
HAPPY 90th MA'AM
I ♥ QUEENIE
CAIRNSTOON.COM /@cairnstoon

A very cross section

Dimbleby: 'Where next?'

Question Time production assistant: 'Dundee.'

Dimbleby: 'Fuck. That place is full of ginger-haired, blue-faced loonies.'

PA: 'Don't worry. We've stretched out the audience catchment area to take in a village in Perthshire.'

Dimbleby: 'I've heard of Perthshire.'

PA: 'Yes, popular with English people who like to shoot things.'

Dimbleby: 'Splendid. What's our studio audience figure for the night?'

PA: 'Two hundred and fifty.'

Dimbleby: 'And the population of this village?'

PA: 'Two hundred and fifty including the idiot.'

Dimbleby: 'Job done.'

FINANCIAL TIMES
BBC SCOTLAND
LEADERS DEBATE
Q HERE
LOL
LOL

The drop

7 MAY 2016

Amid the feverish post-Holyrood election reaction, commentary and ya-boo-suckery, there seemed some confusion as to who the winner was. The SNP, returned to government with 47% of the vote and twice as many seats as their nearest rivals, might be deemed, in any other country, a bit of a shoo-in for that epithet. But this is Scotland, where politics, like the current state of its top flight football, is basically a fight for second place. And that's where the Tories came. Distantly.

What could not be missed, however, was the continuing slide by Scottish Labour towards levels of electoral irrelevance that can only be described as Lib Dem.

(Note to whatever cartoonist first compared the Labour Party to Monty Python's Black Knight: congratulations, you lucky bastard.)

The hearth of Pyrrhus

14 MAY 2016

Relieved, no doubt, to have a story to tell other than SNP supremacy and Scottish Labour rank incompetence, the press nevertheless went just a teensy bit overboard in their paeans to the redoubtable Ms Davidson. To read some of the commentary, you would think Wonder Woman had swapped her indestructible bracelets for a blue trouser suit and deigned to live among us.

Once Parliament reconvened and everyone stopped giggling at Labour sitting on the whoopee cushions the Tories had left on their old seats, reality eventually dawned. Davidson's party, with a smaller portion of the popular vote than even Labour, had won just seven constituency seats compared to the SNP's 59.

The Tories' manifesto talked only of being an effective opposition – they had literally campaigned to lose. Well done, Ruth. You did.

NOW WE'RE IN A POSITION TO HOLD THE GOVERNMENT'S FEET TO THE FIRE.

The History Boys

For a little light relief in these confusing, turbulent times, the Honourable Company of Edinburgh Golfers (HCEG), celebrated guardians of Victorian attitudes and the right to wear offensive trousers, held a vote on whether or not to continue banning half the human race from their club.

Hot on the heels of the Scottish parliamentary election which, as usual, deployed D'Hondt, a voting system everyone agrees is the worst possible apart from all the others, the HCEG's rules stipulated a two thirds majority would be needed before such a radical and frankly absurd proposal could be passed.

To no-one's great surprise, the good old boys voted to stay safe in their make-believe all-male world (although, admittedly, by a narrow margin). When they looked up from their spotted dicks, however, and saw that the actual real world wasn't best pleased with them, they hastily arranged a re-run and decided to leave the 19th century behind after all.

... AND, APPLYING D'HONDT, WE CAN SEE THE MEMBERS HAVE ALSO VOTED TO ABOLISH UNIVERSAL SUFFRAGE, ADOPT THE GOLD STANDARD AND RETAKE SUDAN.

Control freak

Worrying straws in the wind were beginning to blow around down Brexit Way. Cameron and Osborne, having gone for broke with warnings of economic meltdown and no more Eurovision, were not seeing any significant improvement in the poll ratings for Remain. Their answer? More of the same – in fact, the very same threats with the words and numbers moved around a bit.

With the famously Eurosceptical Jeremy Corbyn sitting on his hands, it increasingly fell to others to lead the fight for continued membership of the EU. To her credit, one of the most effective advocates for Remain was Ruth Davidson, who called out the anti-European nutjobs in her own party for the immigration-obsessed, economic illiterates they are. Of course, that was when she was happy to make out she had any principles.

Even Nicola Sturgeon, still enjoying a degree of UK-wide lustre following the previous year's General Election, was roped in to TV debates in an effort to plead the positive case for not abandoning Europe. But some were already beginning to ask themselves: wasn't this supposed to be a foregone conclusion?

I WANT TO TAKE BACK CONTROL!
CAIRNSTOON.COM /@ Cairnstoon

Leading from the back

15 JUNE 2016

UK politicians – including members of Cameron's cabinet – were given free reign to follow their consciences (or blind prejudices) when it came to the EU referendum. But parties did have official standpoints, and Labour's was to back the Remain campaign. I mention this for the record.

In reality the party was all over the place. Alan Johnson led the Labour In campaign but found his efforts constantly undermined by his leader's office, while prominent Labour politicians like Gisela Stuart actively backed the Leave campaign. Some MPs from metropolitan areas were ardent Europhiles, while others from oop nawth – where UKIP were flashing a shapely anti-immigrant ankle at their constituents – frankly didn't know what to say.

And as the Treaty of Rome burned, Jeremy Nero fiddled and footered.

IT'S VITAL LABOUR'S CASE FOR STAYING IN THE EU IS HEARD LOUD AND CLEAR BECAUSE, EH, YOU KNOW ... WHATEVER.

Crocodile tears

19 JUNE 2016

The murder of Labour MP Jo Cox shocked the country. Campaigning in the EU referendum was suspended and the House of Commons was recalled for a special session at which tributes were read out from friends and colleagues. Many MPs from all sides were moved to tears.

News that her murderer was a far-right fanatic with extreme views on immigration was also deeply distressing – even to the far right fanatics with extreme views on immigration editing Britain's tabloid newspapers.

'Where did all this hate come from?' they asked. 'What could this man possibly have read every day for years that would have planted such seeds of evil in his soul?'

PRESS
CAIRNSTOON.COM / @ cairnstoon

Lions and children first

And then the world stood on its head.

The vote for Brexit by 52% came as a shock to everyone. Even Nigel Farage conceded defeat after the polls closed. Only when the early results came in, and the size of the Leave vote became apparent, did the previously unthinkable become all too thinkable.

Scotland had voted overwhelmingly for Remain but once again the laws of British political gravity meant that counted for nought. Britain – and Europe – woke up on 24 June to a new reality, a new normal. It was as if we all lived in a snow globe and someone had just given it a damned good shake.

Cameron resigned, as did half of Corbyn's shadow cabinet, the Bank of England took emergency measures to steady the economy as the stock market crashed, Sturgeon flew to Brussels to meet senior EU figures, and everyone turned to Boris Johnson and Michael Gove and asked what happens now. They grinned back inanely and shoved each other.

'Say something.'

'No, you say something...'

CAIRNSTOON.COM /@ cairnstoon
♪ RULE BRITANNIA ~ BRITANNIA RULES THE WAVES ... ♫
THE JOLLY BREXITEER
INDYREF II

Toga Party

Boris Johnson, having fatally undermined David Cameron and the Remain campaign while ridiculing the notion it was all a plot to have him installed in No.10 as Prime Minister, now prepared to have himself installed in No.10 as Prime Minister. It was a simple matter of gathering his closest friends and allies and presenting himself to the party and the country as the natural choice.

Only it turns out treachery is catching. Hang around Boris for long enough and you start getting ideas above your station. (Shortly after you stop combing your hair and affect a bumbling stutter.)

And so it was that loyal lieutenant and 49-year-old young Tory Michael Gove stabbed the blond fop in the back and announced his own candidacy for party leader and PM.

This was something of a shock coming, as it did, from a man who'd not only said repeatedly that he didn't want the job but, let's be honest, was about as prime ministerial as … oh, I dunno … Andrea Leadsom.

It seemed like a good idea at the time

6 JULY 2016

The nation was given a break from watching the madhouse of current politics by reliving the good old days when all we did was invade countries for no good reason. The Chilcot Inquiry Report into the decision by Tony Blair to go to war in Iraq had taken so long (seven years), and been delayed so often while those investigated got to read it in advance, that a whitewash was widely anticipated. In the event it was damning.

In an address all the more devastating for being delivered in the measured tones of a courtroom lawyer, Sir John Chilcot excoriated Blair's government for rushing to war without exhausting all peaceful solutions, doing so on the basis of dodgy intelligence, ignoring warnings of illegality, and of achieving precisely diddly squat because it hadn't planned for the invasion's aftermath.

Blair himself then gave a bravura performance of sorrowful sincerity (or was it sincere sorrow?) over a two-hour long press conference. What mattered now, he said, was what mattered in 2003 – that he believed it was the right thing to do. It wasn't quite 'Hey, that's why they put rubbers on the end of pencils,' but close enough.

WOULD YOU APPEAR AT
THE HAGUE
TO DEFEND YOURSELF?
DEPENDS.
HOW MUCH DO THEY PAY?
CAIRNSTOON.COM / @ CAIRNSTOON

Hobson's Dilemma

9 JULY 2016

Meanwhile, back in La La Land, the Tory leadership (and de facto prime ministerial) race was now down to just two. Michael Gove and Liam Fox had been reminded nobody likes them and that other guy no-one remembers got his coat and left. It was now just Theresa May, Home Secretary and shoe model, up against Andrea Leadsom, inexplicable star of the Leave campaign and professional mum.

One thing you can say for the Tories – unlike Labour and its now annual summer-long leadership contests: they like to get things over with quickly. The plan was for a decision by early September. In the event, the final head-to-head lasted just days.

Under fire for a CV with more pork in it than a David Cameron university anecdote, Leadsom decided it was time to remind everyone why she was more qualified than May to be Prime Minister, qualified indeed to do anything in the whole wide world: she was A Mother. Anyone left in the Tory Party with a fragment of propriety joined backers of childless Theresa May in condemnation. Mum left the building.

VILLAGE HALL
HOBSON! COME BACK MAN!
TORY LEADERSHIP HUSTINGS
MAY
LEADSOM

Interesting times

16 JULY 2016

The writers of TV soap operas, sitcoms and dramas were not only having a tough time competing with real life, they were having trouble just getting on our screens. Gorging on one major event or disaster after another, news programmes loosened their belts and spread out all over the evening schedules.

While the political circus of post-Brexit vote Britain continued (former shadow cabinet members were now greetin' on camera as they begged Corbyn to quit) the wider world was hardly a refuge of sane normality.

Australians went to the polls and were so unimpressed with any of the parties on offer they voted for nobody in particular and the country went without a government for more than a week. Meanwhile, Turkish generals staged the worst attempt at a military coup since Sgt Major Grout tried to take over Pippin Fort in Camberwick Green by spiking Cpt Snort's tea.

But of course no-one does batshit lunacy quite like the Yanks. A spate of targeted assassinations of police officers across the country wasn't quite enough to keep one story off the front pages: Donald Trump had won the Republican nomination and would be running for President.

AND NOW FOR A SPECIALLY EXTENDED NEWS. SCHEDULED PROGRAMMES WILL RESUME A WEEK ON TUESDAY.

Yeah, whatever

Of course, it was still possible to look at the Trump phenomenon as nothing more than the satirists' gift that kept on giving – not, you know, an actual threat to western democracy and planet Earth. OK, he'd won the Republican ticket but that had been in a contest with cardboard cut-outs and charlatans. Now he was going into a proper presidential election he would be scrutinised as never before, tested in a head-to-head against a genuinely popular, charismatic Democrat with radical, voter-friendly policies and a spotless record of public service.

Unfortunately the Democratic National Committee had other ideas and stitched up Bernie Sanders like a kipper. On the eve of the Democratic National Convention, the party's chair, Debbie Wasserman Schultz, was forced to resign amid allegations of leaning on delegates to get them to back Hillary Clinton.

The scandal wasn't enough to derail the juggernaut that was the Clinton campaign and the DNC duly nominated … the only candidate who could possibly lose to Donald Trump.

CORONATION
FEEL
THE
BERN
US

Slow train coming

30 JULY 2016

The Scottish government's plans to introduce a 'Named Person' scheme (in which every child would be guaranteed access to a designated professional responsible for their welfare) was the subject of a legal challenge in the Supreme Court. But apart from urging ministers to iron out possible infringements of data protection regulations, the top beaks ruled the scheme was pretty much tickety-boo.

Not that you would have discerned as much from the media coverage. The delayed implementation of a child protection scheme with popular, third sector and cross-party support was reported with a quiet restraint and unspun factuality last used to report the Relief of Mafeking.

Never one to knowingly pass up a chance to join a baying, Nat-bashing mob, Scottish Labour attacked the government over the delay in implementing a policy it supported by saying it should be delayed longer. So there.

IN A DEVASTATING BLOW, SCOTRAIL IS FORCED TO ANNOUNCE THAT THE HATED 11:35 FROM EDINBURGH WAVERLEY HAS BEEN STOPPED IN ITS TRACKS. AS A RESULT OF THIS CRUSHING HUMILIATION IT WILL NOW ARRIVE AT 11:55.
CAIRNSTOON.COM / @CAIRNSTOON

Wurrld News

The highly contentious issue of whether or not Scotland could be trusted to talk to itself about anything other than the goings on at Glasgow Sheriff Court reared its head again with a report from the House of Commons' Culture, Media and Sport Committee. Having spent months taking evidence (some of it actually in Scotland!) the committee came down heavily in favour of a 'Scottish Six' on BBC 1, edited and anchored in Pacific Quay.

This would be nothing more or less than a normal news bulletin in which the big stories of the day, be they from Brechin or Beijing, would be reported in descending order of importance and relevance to the audience. It would be followed by the weather. Once.

The recommendation was welcomed by the SNP, broadcasters and anyone not contorted by their cringe into a Gordian Knot of mortified self-loathing.

Speaking of which, Jackson Carlaw, Scottish Tory spokesman on things we shouldn't be allowed to do, warned that the country didn't need an opportunity for the Scottish government to 'shove propaganda down the throats of a dinner-time viewing public'.

How dare he associate the BBC with propaganda.

BBC
WORLD
MURDERS
AND
FOOTBALL

AND NOW FOR
THE NEWS WHERE
YOU URNIE.

Reborn in the USA

The political landscape of post-Brexit vote Britain was still a dangerous place, a seething bear pit of recrimination and score-settling. The country and political parties alike craved stability, cool heads and calm, reassuring leadership. So Kezia Dugdale buggered off to the United States.

Admittedly, the first part of her five week-long sojourn was to attend a leadership course but one might argue (and be joined by Scottish Labour members complaining bitterly in the press) that this smacked of stable doors and horses.

After a visit to the Democratic National Convention where Dugdale warned Americans against voting for that Donald Trump ('Gee, miss – d'you think?') she went on holiday. Meanwhile, her party was splitting into factions supporting Corbyn and Owen Smith, now his only challenger.

She returned to news that Labour was tanking even more in the polls and calls from some of her own members for a formal split with the party south of the Border.

'We'll have none of that,' said Dugdale, now fairly bursting at the seams with leadership skills. 'Once Corbyn's given his jotters, it'll all be just fine.'

HOW DID HER LEADERSHIP COURSE IN AMERICA GO?
MEH...
CUT TIES TO OUR COMRADES SOUTH OF THE BORDER...?
... THAT'S A GODDAMN BUNCH OF BALONEY!
UK LABOUR

Like a well-oiled machine

It was like It's A Knockout was back on the telly – British politics' summer of slapstick fun continued. But if the machinations of the Tory Party, the delusional utterances on Brexit from David Davis (the actual Brexit Secretary) and Nigel Farage's UKIP Dance of the Seven Veils left you yearning for comedy of a less sophisticated variety, there was always Labour's ongoing leadership election to turn to. Because, despite the efforts of the party's desperate wing (previously known as Blairite) it was on-going.

A legal bid to have Jeremy Corbyn prevented from even taking part because not enough MPs liked him was thrown out by the High Court. A more successful barrier was thrown up in the way of a curiously unspontaneous surge in Labour Party membership. Having paid their £25, some 40,000 recent 'converts' to the cause fully expected to be able to vote. Alas, party rules stood in their way … but not in the party's way of hanging on to the thick end of a million quid. Ka-ching!

Meanwhile, at a hustings in Glasgow, Corbyn's challenger Owen Smith obviously thought he was on to a winner by praising local hero Kezia Dugdale. 'She's doing a great job,' he said to a room full of Scottish Labour members.

'Pish!' came the shouted response.

WELCOME TO THE ANNUAL LABOUR PARTY BREWERY PISS UP

GERS: The Movie

Just six months after publishing the 2014-15 Government Expenditure and Revenue Scotland figures, the government decided it was high time the 2015-16 stats should be released. Uncle Tams the length and breadth of the land, still picking their teeth from the last feast of independence on toast, couldn't believe their luck.

The slight problem for unionists this time around was that even these very latest figures took no account of Brexit – a wizard wheeze soon to be imposed on Scotland by the English electorate at an estimated cost to its economy of up to £11 billion a year. The unavoidable truth that GERS is a seriously bad advert for being in a union just got a lot more … truthy.

Of course, the unionist parties and press were only too aware of this which is why, even before this latest GERS publication, they had been screaming blue murder about the prospects of another independence referendum. You could be forgiven for thinking they weren't so sure they would win it.

The CRINGE
SCOTTISH DAILY EXPRESS
30p WE ASK:
WHY WON'T STURGEON JUST ADMIT WE'RE SHITE?
(WITH APOLOGIES TO DR. SEUSS)

Deep Thought

7 SEPTEMBER 2016

The country, having gotten over the shock of what it had voted for in June, turned to those who had egged it on and asked, 'Alright, we did that. What happens now?'

'That's a very good question. Let us think about it for a bit,' came the reply.

In The Hitchhiker's Guide to the Galaxy, Deep Thought, a computer the size of a small city, is built to undertake just one calculation – to explain the meaning of life, the universe and everything. After seven and a half million years it finally answers: 'Brexit means Brexit.'

On a much more mundane level, voters, businesses large and small and governments across Europe simply wanted to know, three months on, what were Britain's proposals for leaving the biggest free market in the world? What was its timetable, its preferred terms and its plan to trade with the rest of the world, to survive?

Had the answer been '42' it could scarcely have been less meaningful.

So to recap, those Brexit details once more:
1) Motherhood;
2) Apple pie.
Any questions?

Our man in Strasbourg

Of particular concern to the unionist chattering classes in the immediate aftermath of the Brexit vote had been the instant collapse of the already ludicrous argument that an independent Scotland would be kicked out of and/or barred from the EU. So much so that the likes of the Daily Mail and Express resorted to telling their readers that what they could see with their own eyes wasn't really happening.

Thus, pictures of the First Minister being warmly welcomed by Juncker, Tusk et al in Brussels, and statements of support and solidarity from senior European parliamentarians, were all clear examples of: 'Sturgeon snubbed'.

One Guy seemed to annoy the yooneratti more than most – Verhofstadt. The MEP and former Belgian Prime Minister had noised them up by forcefully debunking the notion that the EU would ever want to keep an independent Scotland out. And now he was named the chief Brexit negotiator for the European Parliament.

It was almost as if the EU didn't want the UK to have its cake and eat it after all.

MR VERHOFSTADT
WILL SEE YOU
NOW...
BREXIT
NEGOTIATIO

Thanks, Dave

Having said he would be staying in Parliament after resigning as Prime Minister, the man who'd said he wouldn't resign as Prime Minister announced he was leaving Parliament. David Cameron was nothing if not a man of his word. (This is the bit where you draw your own conclusions).

His excuse was that he didn't want to be 'a distraction' to the new Theresa May administration. This was pretty weak stuff because, although he'd taken to sitting on the back benches dressed as Louis XIV and shouting, 'You're all bastards!', MPs were used to it by now. More plausible was that he was going off in a huff, May having sacked all his pals and begun ripping up his programme for government.

And so Dave left the political stage. The man who nearly lost the unlosable Scottish independence referendum then went one better by calling an EU referendum and losing that one. He was, by common consent, the worst Prime Minister Britain had had since Anthony Eden. At least now we had a strong and stable one …

MY WORK HERE IS DONE.
CAIRNSTOON.COM

Hit for six

Worried that a general consensus was forming in favour of an entirely reasonable proposition, the UK government stepped in saying: 'Now then, now then, now then!'

A new Royal Charter for the BBC specified the corporation's role in promoting 'social cohesion' in the context of the 'well-being of the UK as a whole'.

In light of this, government sources called the proposed 'Scottish Six' news broadcast 'dead in the water'. The new charter, they said, 'required the BBC to have a UK-wide approach and to support and promote the United Kingdom'.

'Sources schmources,' said No.10 – officially. 'We're not telling anyone to do anything.'

Shortly afterwards, the Scottish Six was dead in the water. Officially.

But wait. It was then revealed that instead of a poxy wee news programme, Scotland is to have a whole new channel. This will totally not be filled with tartan stereotypes and desperately unfunny sitcoms and will be easy to find on the schedules between Kerrang and That's Carlisle.

And who wants to watch TV before 9pm anyway?

BBC Sco
CAIRNSTOON.COM /@ cairnstoon

Precision bombing

Western allies demonstrated their superior military acumen this month by launching a surgical strike against Daesh militants … and hitting a Syrian Army camp, killing 62 soldiers. The RAF were joined by air forces from the United States, Denmark and Australia in the attack which used drones and laser guided bombs.

It was the worst cock-up on the military front since the UK Parliament had sanctioned striking against Daesh in Syria the previous year. It would have threatened to destabilise the ceasefire in that country had that not already been more honoured in the breach than the observance, and not worth the blood-stained paper it was written on.

Not jumping onto any bandwagon whatsoever was Russia with a call to convene an emergency meeting of the UN security council to discuss an incident it described as 'highly suspicious' and one that 'did not look like an honest mistake'. Twenty four hours later Russia was accused of bombing a UN aid convoy heading for Aleppo, killing at least 20. Nonsense, said Russia, the trucks … 'caught fire'. Happens all the time. Occupational hazard.

Honest mistake, anyone?

OOPS!
SYRIA
CAIRNSTOON.COM /@ cairnstoon

Kez's nightmare

24 SEPTEMBER 2016

The SNP government was on shaky ground with its plans for changes to local government taxation. Too modest for some opposition parties, too radical for others, it looked like a parliamentary motion on the issue would deliver a slap in the face for the minority administration.

To everyone's surprise, however, a vote on a Tory amendment ended in a dead heat leaving the casting vote to the presiding officer who, according to standard protocol, sided with the government. It seems someone had failed to vote.

Thanks to Holyrood's liking for openness and transparency, it wasn't long before the not-so-secret Nat agent was identified – none other than leader of Her Majesty's Reserve Opposition, Kezia Dugdale. 'But I did vote, I did, I did! I pushed the button and everything.'

Denial, however, may as well have flowed through Egypt for all the good it did her; a check of the state-of-the art electronic voting system showed all was in working order.

Never mind, Kez. The results of the Labour leadership election are due this weekend. Your embarrassment will soon be forgotten once Owen Smith wins and your trashing of Jeremy Corbyn is totally vindicated …

AND THE WINNER IS JEREMY CORBYN ...BY A SINGLE VOTE. NOW, ARE WE ALL SURE WE VOTED?

Cicero

The much-anticipated first TV clash between Hillary Clinton and Donald Trump turned out to be less a presidential debate than an argument between a parent and a seven-year-old caught telling fibs. In a rambling and frankly alarming performance, Trump re-wrote history, contradicted himself (sometimes within the same sentence) and made up words.

Donald clearly didn't want to be 'braggadocious' (yes, that's a real word) but he had to point out what a successful businessman he was and therefore knew that the right thing to do was cut taxes 'bigly'. Not as bigly as he'd managed to cut them for himself after admitting that he'd avoided paying any for years. 'That makes me smart,' said the would-be boss of the IRS.

One commentator described his novel approach to answering questions as 'little more than free-associative non-sequiturs'. For example, when pressed on US cybersecurity weaknesses, Trump responded: 'I have a son who's ten. He's so good with computers.'

Somewhere in England, Andrea Leadsom warmed to the Republican nominee.

I HAVE SO MANY GREAT WORDS IT'S UNBELIEVABLE. I DON'T SAY THAT BRAGGADOCIOUSLY (SEE?) JUST BIGLY.
CAIRNSTOON.COM/@CAIRNSTOON

Learning to fall

By the beginning of October – more than three months after the vote – ministers finally decided saying nothing about Brexit was no longer sustainable. So they started talking bollocks instead.

David Davis, the Brexit Secretary, revealed the delusion at the heart of the UK government by saying that, after triggering Article 50 (formal notice to quit), he wouldn't be heading to Brussels to negotiate the divorce but to Berlin to strike a deal that would allow Germans the privilege of continuing to sell us their cars.

This theme was picked up by Foreign Secretary Boris Johnson who said the negotiations would not only be over well inside the two-year deadline but would include a free trade deal, control over immigration, cake and lots of eating.

'We buy more German cars than anybody else,' he said. 'We drink more Italian wine than any other country in Europe, 300 million litres of Prosecco every year. They're not going to put that at risk.'

But it was left to Trade Secretary Liam Fox to give what turned out to be the most accurate hint of the eventual Brexit strategy – one that was out of the single market. Brexit, he said, was a 'glorious opportunity' for Britain to fly free as a free trade bird unencumbered by stuff and nonsense like wings, a parachute or a working knowledge of the laws of gravity.

PAH! WHO NEEDS IT?
I'D SAY IT WAS GOING
SWIMMINGLY SO FAR.
SINGLE MARKET
CAIRNSTOON.COM / @cairnstoon

Silly billy

4 OCTOBER 2016

2016 was not a good year to be a celebrity. If you weren't being exposed in a newspaper sting, facing sexual assault charges or already in jail for interfering with wee boys in the 1970s, there was a fair to middling chance of being dead. The roll call of rock stars, sporting icons and cultural national treasures who cashed in their chips this year was astonishing.

Of course there is always that other pitfall for the famous – making a complete arse of yourself.

John Cleese took exception to a piece by Fraser Nelson in the Daily Telegraph about Sam Allardyce, the then England manager who'd been caught by the same paper demanding £400k speaking fees and offering his advice on how to get around player transfer rules.

Had Cleese limited his comments to a defence of celebrity privacy rights, perhaps no-one would have paid much attention. This, however, was the ex-Python's tweet on the matter: 'Why do we let half-educated tenement Scots run our English press? Because their craving for social status makes them obedient retainers?'

Reacting to the predictable outcry, he then replied: 'It's not casual racism, it's considered culturalism.'

Right you are, John. Thanks for clearing that up.

CAIRNSTOON.COM
@cairnstoon

The Mayfly

Theresa May bestrode the Conservative Party Conference like a colossus. At least she would have if her skirt had allowed more than just a feeble attempt at the George Osborne I've-had-an-accident-in-my-pants power stance. The Tories were feeling good about themselves, and their shiny new leader and Prime Minister was determined to take the credit.

She was also determined to stake a claim to the middle ground of British politics – and the unionist vote, and the soft left Labour vote, the right-wing vote – basically everybody's vote (except perhaps the Greens and Celtic fringe nutjobs).

So she attacked excessive pay at the top of big companies and made a case for state intervention in the market. But she also announced plans for new grammar schools and demanded businesses account for the number of foreign workers they employed. Mostly though, she sought to perform the last rites on UKIP.

'Look, slightly racist fantasists,' she said. 'There's no need to vote for that dysfunctional collection of Farage balloons any more. Brexit is happening and I'm here to tell you it will be just as xenophobic and economically illiterate as you've ever dreamed.'

UKIP

Clear and present danger

22 OCTOBER 2016

When the Daily Record, the paper of 'The Vow', publishes an editorial saying Brexit justifies the SNP pushing for a second independence referendum, you know we're no longer in Kansas, Toto. Of course, unionist politicians had been fully aware of the threat ever since the EU referendum result. They may be unprincipled and disingenuous but they're not thick. (OK, James Kelly is a bit thick, but usually they're not.)

So when Nicola Sturgeon stood up at the SNP conference and announced she would be producing draft legislation for a referendum to be held before the UK (and Scotland with it) quits the EU, the howls of anguish and outrage were as hysterical as they were predictable.

Sturgeon, the yooneratti said, was going off half-cock. There was enough division – what we need now is national healing. Hard Brexit? Says who? Theresa May will listen to the devolved administrations and agree a common approach and, besides, think of all those powers coming back from Brussels that will definitely, cross our hearts and hope to die, go straight to Edinburgh.

Sounds like a vow.

P-PUT DOWN THE
P-PAPER AND
S-STEP AWAY!

INDEPENDENCE
REFERENDUM
BILL

CAIRNSTOON.COM /@ CAIRNSTOON

Trick or treat

28 OCTOBER 2016

While the Scottish government continued to work on proposals for keeping Scotland at least in the single market post-Brexit, the vibes from Westminster were encouraging. Well, they would have been if we weren't dealing with Tories for whom hypocrisy and double standards are categories in their politician of the year awards.

Ordinarily a nod and a wink to the City about a special deal, soothing noises to Northern Ireland about the border with the Republic, and a promise of no tariffs or extra bureaucratic burdens for Nissan's planned fleet of new car production in Sunderland would make Scotland sigh with relief. Here, we should be saying to ourselves, is a government that is willing to listen and accommodate.

Aye, as we actually do say up here, right.

The SNP government's idea of a differentiated Brexit was unrealistic wishful thinking, Tory front benchers opined dismissively. For it to have any chance you'd need to produce a detailed, fully costed and peer-reviewed plan drawn up by a panel of cross-party and professional experts in political theory, EU constitutional law and economics. You'd need to – , what? Oh, you've actually …

Well, you're still not getting it because … reasons.

YEAH, NICE TRY.
GET LOST!
NISSAN
NISSAN
BREXIT
HOUSE

Fork handles

Defenders of British democracy, still flushed with their success in delivering the Brexit vote, were nevertheless keeping a keen eye open for any backsliding. So when a High Court action was raised to preserve our sovereign Parliament's right to approve the formal notice to quit the EU, our patriotic press championed this noble cause with all their usual vim and … no, wait...

The action in question was raised by a 'foreign-born multi-millionaire' so that's a bit suspicious, isn't it? And look at all the garlic-munching remoaners who're supporting it. That can't be good.

No, after careful consideration, our fearless fourth estate decided this development was 'a bad thing'.

So much so that when the court ruled that the government couldn't in fact deny Parliament a say in the matter, the three judges responsible for the ruling were pictured on the front of The Daily Mail above the headline: 'Enemies of the people.'

As thousands of complaints poured into the Independent Press Standards Organisation, parallels were drawn with a 1933 German newspaper which pictured individuals who'd had their citizenship revoked by the Nazis under the headline 'Traitors of the people'.

Pure coincidence, of course. As if The Daily Mail and its owners had any historical links to the Third Reich.

DAILY MAIL
PLEASE.
OK.
WHICH WOULD
YOU LIKE?
Daily Mail
READERS
OFFER

Colour blind

Hard to believe, but the race to elect the 45th president of the United States was finally drawing to an end. Teenagers who hadn't been born when it started asked their parents if the sun would rise as normal on the first day they would know without the election dominating their TV and social media. Would there be anything left to talk about? Would there be Twitter?

Almost as hard to believe was that it was indeed a race. Thanks at least in part to FBI director James Comey grandstanding for a few days on what turned out to be no development at all in the Hillary Clinton email saga, Donald Trump, the sociopathic 70-year-old toddler, was still in with a shout.

But, with intense polling conducted in the final week, an unmistakable 'bounce back' for Clinton was being picked up across a range of organisations. This was proof, the TV studio experts said, of the reality check they had long predicted finally kicking in. Clinton's lead was on average between five and ten per cent. One pollster, SurveyMonkey, which had interviewed more than one million Americans over the campaign, now put her chances of winning at 96%.

Phew!

MAKE AMERICA GREAT AGAIN
I AIN'T NO RACIST.
I'S VOTIN' TRUMP.
AND HE ORANGE.
CAIRNSTOON.COM / @ cairnstoon

The rebrand

Historians will one day write about these astonishing times – the tectonically shifting political landscapes and evaporating certainties. They will – just as soon as they get their heads round this one. But, almost a year on, they can still be found at home staring at their televisions, mouths slightly open.

Donald J Trump became President Elect of the United States after winning enough votes in the US Electoral College system to beat Hillary Clinton to the finishing line. That he lost the popular vote, or 'vote' as it would be known in any sane country, mattered not a jot (except to the man himself who wouldn't stop obsessing about it for months) – the unthinkable, the *impossible*, had happened.

As the entire planet set its affairs in order and stocked up on canned goods, few spared a thought for the Democratic Party. Which was just as it should have been. After eight years of the coolest president since JFK, with a recovering economy and healthcare revolution to burnish its reputation, and up against an incoherent sleazeball, it still managed to lose.

Woo – as they say in America – hoo.

YOU'RE NOT A DONKEY ANY LONGER. FROM NOW ON YOU'RE AN ASS.
DEMOCRATS

Brush strokes

The reverberations of our own political cataclysm were still being felt across the country. In the stormy immediate aftermath of the Brexit vote, Scottish Labour, that most rudderless of vessels at the best of times, had been tossed about the place like a rubber duck in a Jacuzzi. At one point, Cap'n Dugdale even went so far as to say it was 'not inconceivable' she could support independence.

After sober reflection, however, the Labour Party North British Branch Office informed a breathless nation of its new, unequivocal, no this time we really mean it, last word on the constitution. Deputy leader Alex Rowley called for Scotland to enjoy 'home rule in a confederal UK' ('cos, you know, that's totally going to happen) and said he'd never considered himself a unionist.

Asked if she agreed with her deputy on the whole federal thing, Dugdale might've said, 'Absolutely. I'll be banging on about this no end in a few months'. But, not having a crystal ball or a clue, she didn't. What she did say was that Scottish Labour was neither unionist nor nationalist.

Confirmation that SLAB inhabited a parallel political universe, where its ideas and policies had zero effect in this dimension, was at least a comfort to quantum physicists who'd long suspected as much.

RIGHT - LET'S SEE THE NATS GET OUT OF THAT ONE!
BREXIT
CAIRNSTOON.COM / @ cairnstoon

Don't spend it all at once

While the country was busy munching popcorn and watching our political end of the pier show, few noticed that economists, up to their elbows in frogspawn and chicken bones, were looking even more gloomy than usual. Brexit, it would appear, wasn't going to be a skip through the daffodils after all. Inward investment was already declining, borrowing costs increasing, inflation creeping up and growth predictions scaled back.

Without actually using the word 'Brexit', Chancellor Philip Hammond was clearly aware of its looming consequences as he stood up in Parliament to deliver his Autumn Statement. So to keep his audience happy he dished out some goodies – a cancelled rise in fuel duty here, a few million quid to restore a stately home there. But the amateur magician's biggest misdirection was a £23 billion capital stimulus for infrastructure, of which Scotland's share worked out at £800 million.

The tricks didn't end there however because, as is often the case with stuff chancellors pull from their sleeves at the last minute, a little investigation revealed it to be somewhat less than it appeared. Spread over five years, it turns out the new money would only partially offset previous cuts. Scotland's capital spending allowance was still being reduced by almost ten per cent.

Stop it, now. You're spoiling us.

CAIRNSTOON.COM /@ cairnstoon
BREXIT
JUST IGNORE HIM.
HERE, HAVE
A SWEETIE.
£800M

There's no other way

3 DECEMBER 2016

Confusion over the UK's plans for Brexit was by now a wearily accepted fact of British politics. Contradictory statements, insane statements or no statements at all – May's government was deploying them on an almost daily basis to fend off even the most anodyne of questions.

'What will your priorities be once Article 50 is triggered and negotiations begin, minister?'

'Wibble.'

It was no surprise then when Philip Hammond came north to meet the First Minister and ruled out any request from Scotland for a special Brexit deal as 'not realistic' … only for his spokesman to later clarify that as meaning the request would of course be 'carefully considered'.

In truth, no-one seriously expected Westminster to agree to any bespoke deal for Scotland, one that would at least secure access to the single market. Even if the UK government's plans remained clouded in mystery, Scotland's limited options were becoming clearer.

WE'RE RULING OUT EVERY OPTION BUT INDEPENDENCE ~ THUS PROVING ONCE AND FOR ALL THE SNP IS OBSESSED WITH INDEPENDENCE.
YOU'RE SO CLEVER.
CAIRNSTOON.COM / @ cairnstoon

Red, white and blue

At last, the nation had something to work with. We might still not know how extreme Brexit would be, how much it would cost or even when it would start – but at least now we had a colour scheme. It was to be, said Theresa May, a 'red, white and blue' Brexit.

In case anyone thought she was after a good deal for France, she added: 'That is the right Brexit for the United Kingdom.'

She delivered this long-awaited news while on a visit to Saudi Arabia, where she met with a succession of Gulf rulers to discuss trade, security co-operation and how policemen seemed to be getting younger nowadays – anything but human rights, the use of British arms against civilians, bombing Yemen back to the middle ages and suppressing political dissent and a free press.

Was this a sign of things to come, asked anxious NGOs and opposition politicians. Would Brexit Britain be beating a path to anyone in the world who would do business with it, to hell with their democratic credentials or attitudes to race, gender and equality?

'Absolutely not,' said a Downing Street spokesman. 'By the way, you don't happen to have Donald Trump's number do you?'

CAIRNSTOON.COM /@ cairnstoon

All the people all the time

Scottish Finance Minister Derek Mackay unveiled the government's draft budget in the chamber at Holyrood and sat back to bask in the warm applause of his SNP colleagues and reluctant yet honest appreciation by a wrong-footed opposition.

In a surprise development not all of that happened.

It may shock readers to know that your correspondent holds no candle for any political party. Personally, I'd tax corduroy, move the Windsors into a four-in-the-block in The Garngad and legalise throwing dogshit at Tories in the street. But the SNP minority administration had no such freedom of movement and, perforce, produced a raft of proposals designed to satisfy and not enrage in equal measure.

It was therefore a dispiriting confirmation of the state of Scottish politics that the budget induced such a predictably miserable response from Mackay's opposite numbers. The lines of attack were pre-prepared, the outrage over the smallest nuance of taxation overacted to daytime soap levels, and the accusations of timidity rich coming from parties with as much chance of ever being asked to put their policies into action as I have of sending Pickfords round to Buck Palace.

A SHOCKING BUDGET THAT TAXES: TOO MUCH / TOO LITTLE / THE WRONG PEOPLE / MY AUNT SADIE / OUR CREDIBILITY.*
(* DELETE AS APPROPRIATE)
CAIRNSTOON.COM @Cairnstoon

Her Master's Voice

Nicola Sturgeon finally published Scotland's Place in Europe, the report from her Standing Council containing proposals for a differentiated Brexit deal that could give Scotland access to the single market (should the UK leave that, as current Tory rhetoric was suggesting) and retain freedom of movement for EU citizens.

It was not an easy sell to a UK government hell-bent on crushing any dissent on the matter. But, having taken so long to produce and being from such a range of cross-party and no-party expertise, Theresa May was advised from all quarters to listen respectfully to what the report had to say.

Well, at least it wasn't dismissed out of hand. In fact, it wasn't even dismissed after waiting a wee while to make it look like it wasn't being dismissed out of hand. In the event, it wasn't dismissed for three months. But news of this dismissal (in a letter from Brexit Secretary David Davis) wasn't released for another month after that.

The thing was just 49 pages long, so either it had a lot of big words Davis was forced to look up. Or maybe, just maybe, it was used to prop open a door and everyone had forgotten about it.

I LISTEN VERY SERIOUSLY TO WHAT SCOTLAND SAYS. WHAT'S THAT RUTHIE? THE SINGLE MARKET'S FOR SISSIES? YOU KNOW, I THINK YOU'RE RIGHT.
CAIRNSTOON.COM/@CAIRNSTOON

The usual suspects

And so we bade a less than fond farewell to 2016. It was the year when the civilised world stood by helplessly watching as Bashar al-Assad of Syria bombed and poisoned thousands of his own citizens. When Death claimed so many celebrities someone mocked up a Sgt Pepper's album cover … and still couldn't fit them all in.

It was also the year when the Prime Minister thought he could walk on water but went for something just a little less ambitious – curing the Tory Party of its Europhobia. He succeeded only in delivering the greatest peacetime screw-up in British post-war history since – or probably including – Suez. For that, if not just for being outwitted by the talking beer mat that is Nigel Farage, he lost his job.

Usually, the end of a particularly gruesome year brings at least some relief that it is all over and comfort that surely the next one will be better. Usually. With Brexit looming over the country, however, and Donald Trump looming over the world, there was only the fear that we might soon be looking back on 2016 not with relief but yearning for the good old days.

CAIRNSTOON.COM /@ cairnstoon
2016

The only explanation
7 JANUARY 2017

There was a time when allegations of Russian meddling in the US Presidential Election were something of a sideshow. Washington was hanging out the bunting and preparing to accommodate way more people than would actually turn up for the inauguration of The Donald. Everyone else was still practising saying 'President Trump' without laughing hysterically or being a little sick in their mouths.

But, at the risk of coming across as sore losers (as well useless eejits the planet will never forgive) the Democratic Party insisted there was evidence their email servers had been hacked by agents acting on behalf of a foreign power, to wit Russia.

Trump himself had infamously called on Russia to release any incriminating information it had on Clinton during the campaign. Now, the man who would soon be in overall charge of national security wasn't interested in instigating any official investigation into the allegations which, if proved accurate, could lead to charges of treason.

Instead he accused the Democrats themselves then said it could've been Russia, China or a fat kid sitting on his bed in his underpants. Very unpresidential behaviour but all that would change after the inauguration, obviously.

SOMEONE CALLED
KEZIA DUGDALE.
SAYS YOU MUST'VE
HACKED HER EMAILS
LAST YEAR.
CAIRNSTOON.COM/@cairnstoon

Act – geddit?

You remember Scottish Labour's attempt to be all things to all people back in November – when deputy leader Alex Rowley mooted the whole confederal thing? (Come on, pay attention at the back there.) Well, his boss duly jumped on the bandwagon and, a couple of weeks before Christmas, delivered a 'major speech' (she went to London to do it so it must have been) in which she called for a federal UK and a 'new Act of Union'.

Asked in January if Jeremy Corbyn backed this idea, Kezia Dugdale said yes – 'unequivocally'.

'I wouldn't use the words new Act of Union,' Corbyn said a few days later, redefining the term 'unequivocal'.

Dugdale had been equally clear on her opposition to another independence referendum, saying the country was divided enough.

Corbyn, on the other hand, said indyref2 'could be held' if it was voted for by the Scottish Parliament.

The Labour Party there – as ever, pointing in as many directions as possible all at the same time just case one of them turned out to be right.

AN ACT
OF UNION

The sirens

The SNP government duly did what minority governments do – negotiated, compromised and struck a deal to push through its finance bill. The Scottish Green Party extracted £220 million in extra spending (£160 million for local authorities) and supported the government. No animals were harmed in the making of this deal.

Labour and the Tories, however, reacted with such sound and fury you could be forgiven for thinking Patrick Harvie had just returned from Munich with a piece of paper. Of course, their righteous indignation came from opposite ends of the political – sorry, the stupid – spectrum.

Kezia Dugdale angrily accused the Greens of abandoning their radical credentials by not supporting Labour's plan to tax low-income families to compensate for cuts imposed by a UK government they had fought to ensure would be there to impose them.

Murdo Fraser, on the other hand, told his favourite lie about Scotland being the highest taxed part of the UK and berated Finance Minister Derek Mackay for throwing in his lot with 'lentil-munching, sandal-wearing watermelons'.

And once again, Scotland congratulated itself on its modern, grown-up politics and high-calibre lawmakers.

I'M SURE I HEARD SOMETHING THERE.
JUST WIND.
BUDGET

Equal partners

11 FEBRUARY 2017

Forced to formally lay their plans for triggering Article 50 before Parliament in a 'Brexit Bill', the UK government went for the indecent haste approach and crammed debate into as little time as possible (perhaps afraid Labour could at any moment snap out of their trance and remember they were supposed to oppose things occasionally).

One amendment was of obvious interest to Scotland's 59 MPs – the one that would have given the devolved administrations a power of veto over the process. Despite a debate that dragged long into the night, just two of the SNP's 56 MPs were called to speak. At midnight, after waiting several hours, Joanna Cherry finally got to her feet … and was shortly afterwards told to sit down again by Deputy Speaker Lindsay Hoyle. Cue stooshie.

With an outraged Alex Salmond leaping to his colleague's defence, Cherry herself tried to carry on, only for Hoyle to call upon a Tory minister to speak – for the umpteenth time that night.

'I think that the honourable and learned lady's speech has come to an end,' said Hoyle.

Cherry begged to differ and waved several pages of unspoken material at the chair but with no success. It seems Scottish MPs, like children, were to be seen and not heard.

YES, YES - AN INTERESTING
POINT MS. CHERRY.
NOW SIT DOWN AND
WE'LL SEE IF AN ENGLISH
HONOURABLE MEMBER
WOULD LIKE TO MAKE IT.

(THANKS TO RIANA DUNCAN)

Spitting the dummy

The Trump presidency was off to a tremendous start. It was so-o tremendous. It was the best start of any presidency ever. At least that's what the man himself would have us all believe. With the cunning use of your own eyes and ears, however, it was possible to get an entirely different take on the early days of his administration. The truth was that our fears about a Trump presidency were misplaced. The reality was going to be worse – much worse.

Overtly sectarian banning orders for Muslims from his personal selection of 'bad' countries were followed by pledges to overturn Obama's hard-won healthcare reforms. Threats to pull out of the Paris climate change treaty dovetailed with the roll-back of environmental protection laws and promises to 'drill, baby, drill' in the Arctic Circle. Then there was the championing of creationist teaching in schools (as if Trump-voting America wasn't credulous enough already).

And all that's before you get to the bare-faced lying, monstering of the free press and allegations of links to Russians interfering in the previous year's election. The first major casualty of that scandal was National Security Adviser Michael Flynn who was forced to resign … or did so of his own accord … or was fired.

Multiple-choice explanations were by now as close as the White House got to dealing in cold, hard facts.

FLYNN

The welcoming party

Scottish Labour's spring get-together turned into more of a stock car race than party conference, so many car crash TV interviews did Kezia Dugdale have. And – if I may mix my sporting metaphors – it was all down to a couple of 'marquee' signings from south of the Border that made Joey Barton look like a good piece of business.

In these pre-snap General Election days remember, Jeremy Corbyn was still seen as kryptonite to Labour's chances of ever gaining power this side of The Rapture. And, as if to prove my point, less than 48 hours before he was due to speak at the conference, Labour lost the 'unlosable' Copeland by-election to the Tories.

Meanwhile, London Mayor Sadiq Khan, another guest speaker, warmed up his Jock pals by equating Scottish nationalism with racism, causing Kez to take to the airwaves to defend the SNP. And she just loves doing that.

Ah well, at least they could all agree on her great plans for a federal UK with regional assemblies in England and more powers for Scotland and … Jeremy? Sadiq? Hello…?

CAIRNSTOON.COM /@cairnstoon
Scottish
Labour
welcomes
Jeremy
Corbyn

The small print

4 MARCH 2017

The Prime Minister came north to the Scottish Tory conference, the better for us all to see her dancing on the head of a pin. (Certainly the view wasn't obscured by many heads in front – Wee Ruthie's Redoubtables had obviously been reading their own press and booked the SEC Armadillo in Glasgow when, given the numbers that actually turned up, an open mike comedy venue above a pub would have sufficed.)

But back to that pin. The trick the PM was trying to perform was to be seen standing up to SNP demands for more powers for Holyrood post-Brexit, while leaving herself no hostages to fortune. Wouldn't want to limit her options in the future with anything quite so crude as a 'vow', now would she?

And so she attacked the SNP – natch – but in terms the more observant might conclude went beyond the absolutely necessary. She would fight, she said, against a 'looser, weaker UK' post-Brexit. 'We must avoid any unintended consequences for the coherence and integrity of a devolved UK .'

Unintended consequences. Aye, the Tories are good at avoiding those …

* The UK government reserves the right to define the word 'guarantee' to take account of prevailing market and political conditions. Full payment (to be determined) for this guarantee must be made in advance and is non-refundable. The UK government disclaims all conditions, warranties and terms, statutory or otherwise relating to this statement. While every effort has been made to ensure the accuracy of all information, the UK government accepts hee haw liability for any errors or omissions. For full terms and conditions, ask yer da.

The lion's share

11 MARCH 2017

As noted before, the unionist press and opposition parties in Scotland had been immediately aware of the increased 'threat' of independence after the Brexit vote the previous June, and nothing since coming out of Brussels – or David Davis's mouth – had made the prospect any more enticing. What's more, the UK government was still refusing to formally refuse Scotland's request for a differential Brexit deal.

The tension, therefore, was increasing by the day – as was the use of the only line of attack unionists seemed to have left: moaning about how beastly and unpleasant another independence referendum would be.

And so, while the 2014 vote was endlessly recast as a civil war we were lucky to survive, the inventors of Project Fear Mks I and II, the architects of the Brexit vote, the orchestrators of one Tory and two Labour leadership contests (all championed by the hate-peddling Daily Express and Daily Mail) bleated about division.

OH ~ THE DIVISION,
THE DIVISION!

Playmates

With Theresa May expected to formally trigger Article 50 any day, all eyes were on Westminster … until a press conference was called for 11:30am on Monday 13 March at Bute House – official residence of one Ms Sturgeon.

Since the UK government didn't even have the courtesy to reply to Scotland's detailed paper on a bespoke Brexit deal, the First Minister said, it was time for a little hardball: she would be asking Holyrood to back another independence referendum.

It is for precisely such occasions that blue murders, having been committed, are shouted about in the street, and hell, previously restrained, manages to break loose. All of it.

May's signing of the letter to the EU serving official notice to quit was put on hold (despite protests from No.10 that they were always going to wait a pointless two weeks beyond the heavily trailed time). Eventually, the press would get two letter-signing pics – May alone with a Union Jack in the cabinet room signing away Britain's prosperity and influence; and Sturgeon, heels kicked off and curled up on a sofa, drink at her side, formally requesting a Section 30 Order from Westminster for the new referendum.

NOW THAT I'VE REGAINED THE INITIATIVE I HAVE STURGEON EXACTLY WHERE I WANT HER.

Stacking the odds

It was galling. I mean, it wasn't as if the unionist parties hadn't told us often enough what we thought, what we wanted – or, more precisely, what we didn't want. They'd even decreed that one word – 'referendum' – was far too tame, didn't convey enough of its inherent menace and ghastliness. No, from now on the correct term was 'divisive referendum'.

And the media took its cue, using the new form at every opportunity, while skewed questions were asked in polls and skewed results duly produced.

It was a campaign of misinformation and it had lasted for almost a year. The result was that no-one should have been in any doubt whatsoever: Scotland. Did. Not. Want. Another. Divisive. Independence. Referendum.

There was, however, one teensy weensy problem: it did.

Not with any great enthusiasm, it must be said, and not immediately – but then, no-one was suggesting that. Once the Brexit deal (or no deal) had been arrived at, however, and the choice facing Scotland was clear, then yes, the majority said in every fairly worded poll, please allow us to make that choice. So the pro-independence majority the public had elected at Holyrood voted to do just that. Democracy's a bugger innit?

OUR MANDATE IS BIGGER THAN YOURS.

Give 'em enough rope

And so the deed was finally done. Theresa May's letter triggering Article 50 was duly delivered to European Council President Donald Tusk. There was no going back now – well, not for Maidenhead any way.

Asked in Parliament by SNP Westminster leader Angus Robertson about how she planned to accommodate Scotland's resounding vote to remain as part of the EU, May replied that her own constituency of Maidenhead had also voted to remain – so, you know, tough.

True to form for this increasingly crass and tone-deaf government, even writing a letter couldn't be pulled off without controversy. The text contained a thinly veiled threat: give us a good deal on trade or you can kiss goodbye to co-operation on security. This in the wake of the Paris, Nice, Brussels, Berlin and, indeed, Westminster attacks.

Stay classy, Britain.

WHEEE!!
CAIRNSTOON.COM /@cairnstoon

The levers of power

New figures having revealed the Scottish economy retracted in the last quarter of 2016, SNP government ministers sighed, took their tin hats out from the bottom drawer of their desks and put them on. The flak, they knew, would be heavy.

Like all flak, however, it was also wild, indiscriminate and inaccurate. Ignoring mere details like the effect of the Brexit vote (even though their counterparts south of the Border had no such qualms with regards to the UK economy as a whole) and the fact that Edinburgh has as much control over Scottish macro-economic policy as Clackmannanshire, opposition parties pounded the government. It was all the fault of the SNP's obsession with independence, they averred.

In other words: 'Your campaign to acquire real economic controls is adversely affecting the economy. And while we're at it, what precisely are you going to do about it? And don't give us that "we don't have any controls over the economy" rubbish – we've covered that.'

IT'S STALLING.
DO SOMETHING!

True colours

To be fair to the Scottish mainstream media, they weren't the only ones captivated by the obvious charms and heavyweight political talent (it says here) of Ruth Davidson. Their London counterparts saw a star in the making and took every opportunity to big her up – even (whisper it) as a future UK party leader. But then, we always knew they paid precious little attention to what happens in Scotland.

Because what was happening was that a dark and rather unpleasant secret about Ruth Davidson was being (re)discovered. She's a Tory.

This awful truth came to light over the so-called 'rape clause' – a mean and cruel policy requiring women to prove they'd been raped before getting benefits for a third child. Any right-thinking, poor-hating, I'm-alright-Jack Conservative would be perfectly at ease with it. And that's what Davidson was – despite managing to look almost guilty during the Holyrood debate on the issue (featuring a *tour de force* by Kezia Dugdale, it must be said).

Social security being a reserved matter, Scottish taxes are also therefore reserved by Westminster to pay for it. So using Holyrood's new and limited benefit powers in this case to effectively cancel out the policy would mean costing Scottish taxpayers even more, one way or the other.

And Davidson's response to Scotland's moral outrage?

'Boo hoo. Put your money where your conscience is.'

NOT RAPED? PITY ~ 'COS NOW YOU'RE MUGGED. I CAN'T BELIEVE THE SNP DON'T PUT A STOP TO THIS.
CAIRNSTOON.COM
@cairnstoon

Geronimo

On the morning of Tuesday, April 18, No. 10 asked the media to foregather in Downing Street for an announcement by Prime Minister Theresa May. Such was the febrile state of British politics that speculation among the press corps ran from her resignation on the grounds of ill health to calling off Brexit as a practical joke that had now gone on long enough because literally no-one in the country was laughing any more.

'A General Election?' asked someone. 'Nah, don't be daft.'

But a General Election it was. Despite a solid majority won just two years previously, and an official opposition that took their hands off each others' throats only long enough to vote for or abstain on whatever the government was doing, May decided she wanted more. What could possibly go wrong?

The first hurdle to said election, however, was the small matter of the Fixed-term Parliaments Act. Only the agreement of two thirds of MPs in the House could allow a snap election – meaning the government would need the support of the Labour Party. A Labour Party with an unelectable leader and registering somewhere below gastroenteritis in the opinion polls.

So of course they agreed to it.

Insanity. It's catching.

Labour
COMING THROUGH!
BREXIT

For their queen
and their country

Local elections are the wallflowers at the nation's democratic dancehall – tapping their feet while watching the general elections and nationwide referenda get all the attention, desperate for that one fleeting chance to get onto the dancefloor and strut their stuff. The 2017 Scottish Local Government Elections, however, managed to grab everyone's attention – by pretending to be about anything other than local government.

Thanks to the ceaseless unionist anti-indyref2 onslaught (I may have mentioned this before) the only topic for discussion was the prospect of another 'divisive referendum'. Bin collections and leisure centre car parking charges never got a look in.

A consequence of this was a surprising spike in Tory councillors elected in some of the most deprived areas of the country … surprising until the Orange Lodge started crowing about the number of its members (nameless, of course) who had been elected to 'defend the union'. Good luck with that at the Waste Management and Recycling Sub-Committee.

Meanwhile, the SNP suffered another 'humiliation' … by coming first in every major city and winning 155 more seats than any other party – five times its winning margin in 2012. How many more such drubbings could the party take, concerned media pundits asked.

CAIRNSTOON.COM / @cairnstoon
FOOD BANK
THIS IS ALL
PERFECTLY FINE.

Kim Jong May

13 MAY 2017

The Conservative Party (including most of the Cabinet) had been just as surprised as anyone else by May's decision to go for a snap General Election. So while they and opposition parties huddled in back rooms to cobble together manifestos that didn't look and smell like re-boiled versions of policies they were already serving up, the bold leaderene headed out into the country to sell her message directly to the commonality.

And the message was: 'Strong and stable.' One might have added 'Any questions?' at the end there for comic effect but questions weren't actually allowed, at least from anyone who might ask a tricky one like: 'Do you have anything to say other than "strong and stable"?'

This mind-numbing mantra of patronising piffle was repeated again and again in front of carefully selected, placard-waving audiences across the land – a roadshow of such insulting arrogance even Laura Kuenssberg of the BBC felt moved to challenge it … and was promptly dropped from the approved list of 'most favoured journalists'.

Theresa May, her apologists argued, was a 'get the job done' type of person. She just wasn't comfortable with public speaking, debates or meeting ordinary people. Lucky she didn't go into politics then.

CAIRNSTOON.COM /@cairnstoon
OK~ NOW I'M WORRIED.
KIM JONG UN'S COUNTRY
NORTH KOREA

Bedfellows

Almost three weeks on from the Scottish local elections and the political hue of local governments in much of the country was yet to be determined. The single transferrable vote system had produced, as it usually does, an inconclusive set of results requiring coalitions and working majorities to be formed.

The added complication this year was that the SNP and Labour nationally were engaged in a 'who hates the Tories more' competition.

The SNP came out with most seats in 16 of Scotland's 33 local authorities … but in three of those it didn't even get a chance to form an administration. Because, despite a prohibition ordered by Kezia Dugdale, the most authoritative politician of her generation, local Labour members in Aberdeen, West Lothian and North Lanarkshire decided they would indeed sup with the devil. The entire Labour Group on Aberdeen City Council was eventually kicked out of the party, but fellow rebels in Lanarkshire and Lothian, though equally determined to relive those heady Better Together days with their Tory pals, were a bit smarter. They went into coalition without calling it a coalition – voting each other into all the key chairman and convenor posts.

It walked like a duck and talked like a duck but it was in fact an Early Flemish Triptych Altarpiece of the 15th century Ghent-Bruges School heavy in biblical symbolism and anyone who says different is a dirty lying Nat.

I MIGHT HAVE
TO TAKE THIS
OFF FIRST.
SUITS ME.

The human shield

One of the most benighted General Elections in living memory was thankfully drawing to a close. Called in the wake of the Westminster Bridge terror attack, two other atrocities during the campaign – at the Manchester Arena and London Bridge – had made the country nervous and anxious for brave and principled leadership. Remarkably, that looked more likely coming from Jeremy Corbyn than Theresa May.

A Tory campaign that had begun self-satisfied and lacklustre had only gotten worse. Twice the robotic PM had been switched off and back on again in 'campaign relaunches' but she still operated with all the easy grace of a speak-your-weight machine with dodgy wiring.

In particular, her refusal to expose herself to anything but the most controlled situations – stage-managed rallies and one-to-one interviews in which she refused to answer a single question – was backfiring spectacularly. When she dodged a TV leaders' debate, sending instead Home Secretary Amber Rudd (who had lost her father just days before) something snapped in the nation's patience with this most aloof of prime ministers.

SHE, EH...
COULDN'T
MAKE IT.

The pitch

In Scotland, the General Election, like the local elections before it, didn't do what it said on the tin. Was it a verdict on austerity, on how Westminster is treating Scotland, the prospects of a Labour government any century soon, Brexit...? No – this election, according to the unionist parties and a media, as ever only too willing to dance to their tune, was about two things: the SNP's record in government, and our old friend, the d******e referendum.

The competence of the governing party in Scotland is of course a fair enough topic for discussion … up to a point. It was a point, however, that many in the media were only too happy to overshoot. Even in TV leaders' debates an exasperated Nicola Sturgeon found herself reminding host and opponents alike that this was not a Holyrood election and, important as education reform or Scotrail's performances were, they weren't going to be troubling the lawmakers of Westminster.

As for indyref2, Sturgeon had a wee bombshell up her sleeve which she dropped right into Kezia Dugdale's lap in the last STV leaders' debate. It was the revelation that they'd spoken immediately after the Brexit vote and Dugdale had admitted Labour might well support a second independence vote. Davidson pounced like a cat on a wounded speug as Dugdale spluttered but, tellingly, didn't deny.

(She did later – but presumably only after asking lots of people if they thought she should.)

So REMEMBER ~ LET'S GET OUT THERE AND VOTE AGAINST
A GOVERNMENT THAT ISN'T STANDING BECAUSE OF STUFF
THAT ISN'T RELEVANT SO YOU GET A GOVERNMENT YOU
DON'T WANT AND WE CAN STOP YOU HAVING A CHOICE
IN A FEW YEARS WHEN YOU'LL REALLY NEED IT.
YOU KNOW IT MAKES SENSE.

The lame duck

Theresa May was later to admit that, as the first results came in during the early hours of June 9, she shed a tear. It was just one of many that were being shed that night because the country was pissing itself laughing. The strong and stable leader, the safe pair of hands, had gambled … and lost.

Expected at the outset of the campaign by most commentators to win a majority of around 200, she instead managed to lose 13 seats and with it any majority at all.

As an incredulous country gazed upon the aftermath of yet another political catastrophe, the hours were being counted down until surely a discredited, miscalculating, inept and risible Prime Minister resigned in ignominy. But wait, who is this riding over the horizon on a white charger, orange sash a-flutter?

Yes, it seems Theresa May had even more depths to plumb. The woman who had scared the children with horror stories of a Labour government propped up by the 'dangerous nationalists of the SNP' was now going to beg those nice dinosaur-denying folks of the Democratic Unionist Party to keep her in No.10.

The attainment gap

17 JUNE 2017

The result of the General Election north of the Border was, as usual, one requiring a quite different interpretation and analysis. The unionist parties all made gains at the expense of the SNP who, after the tsunami election of 2015, shipped 21 seats, including those of some big names in the party – Alex Salmond and Angus Robertson chief among them. It was not a good night for the Nats.

The Tories were the biggest beneficiaries, increasing their Westminster contingent from Fluffy Mundell to a football team plus a couple of subs. Even the Lib Dems, though registering a drop in their share of the popular vote, still managed to pick up a few seats. As for Labour, their performance was lauded as the best comeback since Lazarus; Ian Murray was no longer Billy No Mates.

OK, it was probably actual Labour supporters who'd voted for Labour candidates in other seats (as opposed to Tories for torn-faced of Morningside) and the gains were undoubtedly part of the UK-wide Corbyn bounce – despite Murray and Dugdale being sworn enemies of their party leader. But, come on – two years ago they had 41 seats and now they have seven. Woo-hoo.

35
13
7
4
NO, NO, NO. LET'S TRY THAT AGAIN, SHALL WE? WHICH OF THESE IS THE LARGEST NUMBER?
EDUCATION REFORMS
WWW.CAIRNSTOON.COM
@ cairnstoon.

Come on Arlene

Two weeks after the General Election and the country was still without a functioning government. In a shocking development, Theresa May was discovering that a thing she thought would be a doddle was anything but. After Brexit and skooshing a General Election, now it was negotiating a deal with Arlene Foster's DUP.

The wily Arlene, you see, had been here before; wheeling and dealing is a way of life in Northern Irish politics. Theresa, on the other hand, was used to just relying on her Cruella De Vil shtick to scare people into doing what she wanted. Belfast protestants, she was discovering, don't scare so easy.

Eventually, the woman who says she'll be a tough Brexit negotiator (a 'bloody difficult woman') lost the last shreds of her political reputation, endangered the Northern Ireland Peace Process and enraged Scotland and Wales further (if such a thing were possible) – and all it cost her (us) was £1.5billion.

At this rate we'll be lucky to get out of the EU with our trousers.

TALK TO
THE HAND.

A pleasure shared

A Fraser of Allander Institute report predicted two consecutive quarters of negative growth for the Scottish economy – and a Dad's Army of Private Frazers prepared to revel in the gloom, doom and disaster. So eager were Scottish Labour and the Tories to beat each other to the feeding frenzy they sent their press releases excoriating the SNP government to newspapers a day in advance.

But the actual figures released by the Treasury were a pleasant surprise. The Scottish economy in fact grew in the first quarter of 2017 – and by four times the rate of the UK economy as a whole. Manufacturing output was up, as was industrial activity in the North Sea sector for the first time since the oil price crash. It was a bitter blow for the opposition.

But they made the best of it. Scotland, they said, had been 'dragged half way to recession', the economy was 'erratic and patchy'. It was probably only a temporary respite because, as everyone knows, Scotland is fundamentally a basket case … which, of course, we are proud to live in and how dare you accuse us of talking the country down.

BBC
THE END IS NIGH
CANCELLED
I AM OF COURSE DELIGHTED.

The power grab

Brexit Secretary David Davis finally published the Great Repeal Bill, the necessary legislative measure for ensuring there would be no legal black hole once the UK left the EU. To no-one's surprise, it didn't contain provisions for passing powers directly to the devolved administrations.

In fact, in a further slap down for the 21st century and its trendy redistributive notions, it seems Henry VIII, that great democrat, would be making a comeback in the form of his eponymous powers the government wanted to use to bypass Parliament. You know, for efficiency's sake.

It was all a far cry from the promises of vast new powers for Holyrood made by Scottish Secretary David Mundell. But then, real life usually was a far cry from anything Fluffy said. (He was already getting all shouty and defensive over the fact he'd promised Scotland oodles of cash on the back of the government's grubby deal with the DUP.) The reality was that, if unamended, the Grabby McGrabface Bill would leave Edinburgh and Cardiff effectively frozen out of whole swathes of responsibilities they currently hold.

Oh, so *that's* what you meant by 'taking back control'.

GRAB?
WHAT MAKES YOU
THINK IT GRABS?
GREAT
REPEAL BILL
CAIRNSTOON.COM /@ cairnstoon

Happy holidays

Formal Brexit negotiations with the EU having been on the go for a few weeks, it was perhaps time to check on progress. Well, let's see:

The status of EU citizens in Britain and British expats in Europe? *Pending*.

Britain's exit bill to take account of shared assets and liabilities? *Pending*.

Preserving an open border between Northern Ireland and the Republic? *Pending*.

The exact terms of a new trading relationship between Britain and the EU? *Pending in lieu of all of the above*.

And by 'pending' I really mean 'anyone's guess'. That was certainly the view of EU chief negotiator Michel Barnier who, in a series of press briefings, couldn't – and didn't even try to – hide his frustration at the lack of progress. His comments on the British position was summarised thus: what position?

One picture released prior to a session of talks spoke volumes. There was Barnier and his team on one side, documents, position statements and supporting material in neat, thick piles. Opposite sat David Davis and his team bringing nothing to the table but stupid grins.

CAIRNSTOON.COM / @cairnstoon
BREXIT
IS SO BRACING

The McCain Mutiny

It was, pundits agreed, the worst week of the Trump presidency so far. And that was saying something.

Although perhaps the most significant and substantive development, Senator John McCain leaving his hospital bed, where he was being treated for brain cancer, to cast the decisive vote thwarting Trump's efforts to repeal the Affordable Care Act was almost lost amid the vaudevillian omnishambles the administration was descending into.

As the Russia investigation net closed in on his son and son-in-law, occasioning rare and uncomfortable public appearances from them both to deliver far from convincing declarations of innocence, Trump declared Twitter war on his attorney general. And, in two of his most ordurous public speaking appearances to date, he turned a boy scout jamboree into a rambling self-promoting political rally, and told police officers that beating up suspects was OK with him.

Meanwhile, builders were being called out to fit a revolving door to the West Wing: White House spokesman and accidental national treasure Sean Spicer out; new communications director, Anthony 'Ba-da-bing' Scaramucci in; Chief of Staff Reince Priebus out; new CoS General John Kelly in; Scaramucci out again.

Reality TV was never so unreal.

SEE WHAT HAPPENS WHEN EVERYBODY HAS ACCESS TO HEALTHCARE?

Brexit Puppies

5 AUGUST 2017

The Brexit fairy tale was slowly unravelling. The first fib to be exposed, of course, had been the infamous pledge on the side of the Leave campaign's battle bus to take £350 million-a-week currently handed over to the EU and give it to the NHS instead. (Editor's note – the only accurate bit of that is that there was a bus.) But the growing suspicion was that the government's determined vagueness about all things Brexit was only partly to cover up the fact they really didn't know what they were doing.

It was also to avoid admitting that rather a lot of their wild promises about a glorious-once-more Albion were undeliverable in the real world. At the time of writing, the tiresome three shell game about the single market, customs union and freedom of movement was still being played by cabinet minsters in the media (believe the last one you heard at your peril).

Meanwhile, industry sectors and special interest groups who had been cheerleaders for 'taking back control' were being let down one by one. Farmers were already smarting after being told there was no guarantee of EU-size subsidies coming their way from London, nor that they'd have the migrant workers they depend on.

Now it was time for those staunchest of pro-union, anti-EU types – the trawlermen – to have their bubble burst. Danish, and probably Spanish, boats would indeed still have access to British waters post-Brexit, a sheepish Michael Gove was forced to admit on a visit to the North East.

Honestly, you can't trust anyone these days.

YES, THEY
SOLD ME ONE
OF THOSE TOO.

Bread and circuses

The last days of a politically bankrupt Roman republic saw politicians buying off a cynical populace – the 'mob' – with free wheat and hugely expensive games in the arena. Any comparison with 21st century Britain would, of course, be wildly inappropriate. For one thing, no-one's giving out anything for free and, for another, it's the politicians themselves who are the circus act.

But, oh, how our elected leaders would love to have something – anything – they could use to divert our attention away from the monumental cock-up they are making of running the country. As I write, it is deep into the summer of 2017 and the annual 'silly season' of slow news, no news and what Trump would call fake news. It is, we all know, the calm before the storm. Dark clouds are gathering over Brexit Britain (and Trump's White House for that matter). Only the most delusional of alt-right optimist thinks this is all going to end well.

As far as the metropolitan centre is concerned, Scotland has gone from being the major constitutional story of the age to something of an afterthought. Unionist commentators like to convince themselves that London has won the game of chicken with Edinburgh, that indyref2 is off the table. Aye, right.

We have witnessed nothing more than the 'jockeying for position' at the start of Wacky Races. So, buckle up, folks.

My final thanks for your support and for keeping Wings – and all the other pro-independence media – read, watched, shared and funded. It is that level of support, more than anything else, that worries the bejesus out of our opponents. Let's keep them worried 😉

Contents

Also available from cairnstoon.com

Welcome to Cairnstoon

PUBLISHED 2015

"His cartoons and illustrations helped make Wings Over Scotland the most influential opinion-former of the referendum campaign." Kevin McKenna, The Observer.

"Mr Cairns pens a weekly cartoon for my website, Wings Over Scotland. Whether it's a caricature of some hapless politician or a depiction of the readers' beloved, big-pawed lion mascot Hamish, it's a sign that the weekend has arrived and everyone can relax a bit." Rev. Stuart Campbell, Wings Over Scotland.

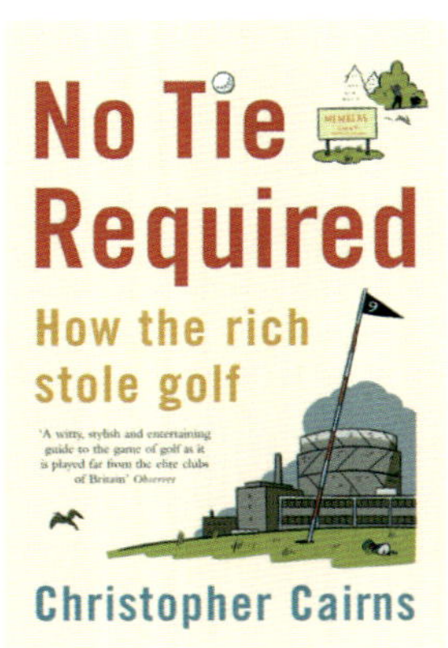

No Tie Required

PUBLISHED 2005

Shortlisted for British Sports Book of the Year, 2006.

"A witty, stylish and entertaining guide to the game of golf as it is played far from the elite clubs of Britain." The Observer.

"Required reading." Golf Punk magazine.

"I enjoyed and was informed by this easy, entertaining book … delightful." Graham Spiers, Scottish Review of Books.

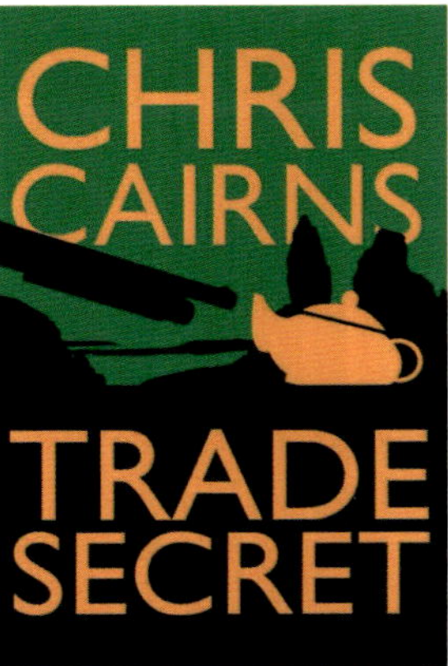

Trade Secret

PUBLISHED 2013

'Trade Secret by Chris Cairns is a clever, funny and enthralling thriller firmly and authentically set in the island of Skye … It is implausible. But it works just fine. The baddies make you want to boo, there are more twists and turns than on the old Sleat road, it is much better written – and more securely grounded – than some other recent examples of Hebridean noir, and far from losing his grasp of his subject and his place, Chris Cairns's sheer enjoyment in writing Trade Secret infects the reader and draws us in.' – Roger Hutchinson